Does It Matter?

The Biblical Text and Bible Versions

E. Allen Griffith, DD

Prepared for classroom use at
Keystone School of Biblical Theology
Lebanon, Pennsylvania

Does it Matter?

© 2013 by E. Allen Griffith
ISBN: 978-1-937129-90-3

E. Allen Griffith, DD
Biblical Family Ministries
P. O. Box 285 • Myerstown, PA 17067

Published by Faithful Life Publishers
3335 Galaxy Way • North Fort Myers, FL 33903

www.FaithfulLifePublishers.com
info@FaithfulLifePublishers.com

Scripture quotations are from the Authorized King James Version of the Bible. Other translations are used to illustrate discrepancies.

Printed in the United States of America
18 17 16 15 14 13   1 2 3 4 5

Does It Matter?

The Biblical Text and Bible Versions

Introductory Thoughts

For many years Bible believing Christians trusted and used the King James Version of the Bible for preaching, teaching, and memorizing Scripture. In more recent years there has been a virtual avalanche of English versions produced, marketed, and accepted by many believers and their churches.

Beneath the publication and marketing of these versions is an ongoing discussion and debate over the New Testament Greek Manuscripts, which have been used as a basis for translation. The King James Version comes from one Greek Text (often called the TR, the Received Text, or the Traditional Text); while every other version comes from other Greek Texts, which themselves are often eclectic. Eclecticism, generally speaking, is the process of following a reading from one manuscript in one place while following other manuscripts in other places. With Eclecticism being practiced, it is no wonder we have so many English versions available.

Our study only introduces the issues of the debate, but is intended to demonstrate why a strong minority of Bible believers are not willing to reject the Traditional Greek Text or willing to accept the newer English versions.

Does it matter?

Early Translations of the Bible into English

The first efforts to translate portions of the Bible into English can be traced back to the 700s, but most people are more familiar with the later work of John Wycliffe in the 1380s. These early efforts were translations from the Latin Vulgate, not from Hebrew and Greek.

In 1525 William Tyndale translated the Scriptures into English, with the distinction that he worked from the original languages—Hebrew for the OT and Greek for the NT. He did his New Testament translation using Erasmus' third edition of his Greek text dated 1522. Tyndale also had a copy of Luther's German New Testament.

The work of Miles Coverdale came next. His translation work into English (1535) provided us with the first printed edition of the Bible, which included all 66 books. He revised Tyndale's work, but used the Latin Vulgate as well as Zwingli's Zurich Bible (a work in German apparently based on the work of both Luther and Erasmus) and Luther's German Bible (translated from the Greek text, using Erasmus' second edition in 1519).

The translation of greatest influence until the King James Version was the Geneva Bible, printed in 1560. The Geneva Bible was translated from the original languages; but perhaps relied on Tyndale's work, as 80% of the Geneva Bible's language is in agreement with Tyndale. The Geneva Bible was the first to use verse divisions and also provided other helps to the reader.

Finally, for the purpose of this section of discussion, came the King James Version of the Bible. It was also translated directly from the original languages—Hebrew and Greek. The Greek text was Beza's Greek Testament (mainly his 4th edition c.1588). The title page of the 1611 translation of the King James Version says, *The Holy Bible, containing the Old Testament and the New: Newly translated out of the original tongues and with the former translations diligently compared and revised; by his Majesty's special commandment; Appointed to be read in Churches.*

The *former translations* mentioned on the title page and used by the KJV translators included the English works of Wycliffe, Tyndale, Coverdale, as well as the unpopular Bishop's Bible—along with Latin, Spanish, French, and Italian translations. We will note here that Beza's work (though he had a large collection of materials from which to work) rarely departs from the 4th edition of Stephanus' Text (1551). And the 4th edition of Stephanus' Text agreed closely with the 5th edition of Erasmus (1535). **One can notice that all the translations of the New Testament from Greek into English, up to and including the King James Version, can be traced back to the work of Erasmus.**

The Traditional Greek Text

Erasmus was born in Rotterdam, Netherlands in 1466. Among other successes, he was considered a genius and the most famous scholar of his day in Europe. He mastered Latin and Greek and taught at various educational levels all over the continent. In 1515 he visited Basel (Basle), Switzerland to prepare a Greek text of the New Testament. It was published in1516. Between the years of 1516 and 1535, he published 5 editions of the New Testament. As a basis for his translation, he found 5 manuscripts at Basel which have been dated to the 12th century—some say as far back as the 8th century.

Some sources say he used 7 or more Greek manuscripts, and apparently used some Latin manuscripts as well. All that he used were representative of the text found in the vast majority of Greek manuscripts extant (known) at that time.

*Information found in Hills' *The King James Version Defended* pgs.198-99, and supported in other materials, reveals 5 manuscripts used by Erasmus; designated as 1, an 11th century manuscript of the Gospels, Acts and the Epistles; 2, a 15th century manuscript of the Gospels; 2ap, a 12th – 14th century manuscript of Acts and the Epistles; 4ap, a 15th century manuscript of Acts and the Epistles and 1r, a 12th century manuscript of Revelation. Hills acknowledges there were other Greek manuscripts. Detroit Baptist Seminary Journal in their article, "Erasmus and the Textus Receptus, " lists Codex 2e from the 12th century and Codex 7p from the 11th century.

Erasmus died in 1536. Robert Stephanus (Robert Estienne) (1503-1559) took up the work of publishing Greek editions of the New Testament. Stephanus produced 4 editions dated in 1546, 1549, 1550, and 1551. Hills, pg. 204 quotes Souter— Williams in stating that Stephanus' 3rd and 4th editions agree closely with Erasmus' 5th edition.

Theodore Beza (1519-1605) produced 10 editions of the New Testament. *Hills pg. 206,* tells us that while Beza had many sources available to him, *Beza in his text rarely departs from the 4th edition of Stephanus.* As noted above, the King James Version was based mainly on Beza's 4th edition.

The Elzevirs—Bonaventure, Matthew, and nephew Abraham, published Greek New Testament editions in 1624 and 1633. They followed Beza, but included input from Erasmus' work, the Latin Vulgate, and the Complutensian. The Complutensian was a Polyglot Bible produced at the Complutense University in Madrid, Spain in 1514, but not immediately published. The term *polyglot* refers to a Bible which contains the same text in several different languages.

As noted earlier, all English versions of the New Testament, up to and including the King James Version, can be traced back to the Traditional Greek Text and the work of these scholars.

Public Rejection of the Traditional Text and the King James Version

In 1870 the Church of England appointed a committee to revise the King James Version. The committee produced the English Revised Version, which was published in 1881. This work in England was paralleled by a cooperative work in America, which produced the American Standard Version in 1901. These two versions were eventually supplanted by the Revised Standard Version of 1946.

The so called revision of the King James Version was actually motivated by a rejection of the Traditional Greek Text on which the King James Version was based. It was the text which had been used and accepted by Christian scholars for hundreds of years. Behind the revisionist efforts were two men who worked successfully to undermine confidence in the Traditional Text, known as the Textus Receptus. They were Constantine Tischendorf and Samuel Tregelles. In turn, those men had tremendous impact on Brook Foss Westcott and Fenton John Anthony Hort.

In 1851, Fenton Hort wrote of his antagonism toward the Textus Receptus and determined to produce a new edition of the Greek New Testament. Though it took 28 years to complete the work, in 1881 Westcott and Hort published *The New Testament in the Original Greek.* It was this Greek text, along with critical work from Edwin Palmer, Tregelles, and Tischendorf, which became the primary sources for the translation of the English Revised

What was offered as a revision of the King James Version made over 30,000 changes in the New Testament, but 5,337 of them were made in direct rejection of the Traditional Greek Text. **In other words, those who *revised* the King James Version were actually undermining its underlying Greek foundation. Publishing the English Revised Version represented a rejection of the Traditional Greek Text and the King James Version.**

The Later History of the Traditional Greek Text

It is important at this point of our discussion to understand more about the Greek manuscripts used by Erasmus, Stephanus, Beza, and the Elzevirs, so we can have a better understanding of their various editions and why we would consider them authoritative for translation into English. Also we must consider why any of the translators would consult the Latin Vulgate.

From the 4ᵗʰ century AD forward, there was an expansion of the presence and use of the Traditional Text—though it is evident that other texts existed as well. Whatever competition there may have been among texts to gain acceptance by Christians, the Traditional Text became the accepted text or, as some would call it, the Received Text. The term, *Received Text* (Textus Receptus), was first used in the preface of the Elzevirs' 2ⁿᵈ edition of their Greek New Testament.

Until the middle of the 4ᵗʰ century, there were a number of texts being used in the Syrian church. After that time they turned to the ancient Peshitta Syriac Version, which primarily follows the Traditional Text manuscripts. *Peshitta* means simple or common. The earliest version now available is dated to the 5ᵗʰ century.

Later in the 4th century (382 AD), the Latin Vulgate was produced by Jerome in response to a request by Pope Damascus. Jerome claimed that he worked by comparing the *Old Latin* version with *Old Greek* manuscripts. A. F. J. Hort (who we will discuss later) stated in his *New Testament in the Original Greek, Vol. II*, pg 152, *By a curious and apparently unnoticed coincidence, the text of A in several books agrees with the Latin Vulgate in so many peculiar readings devoid of Old Latin attestation, as to leave little doubt that a Greek manuscript largely employed by Jerome in his revision of the Latin version must have had to a great extent a common original with A.*

Codex **A,** to which Hort refers, is the designation for manuscript Alexandrinus—so named for having come from Alexandria. Codex **A** follows the Traditional Text in the Gospels. Hort's statement acknowledges that the Old Greek manuscripts used *largely* by Jerome in producing the Latin Vulgate were partly of the Traditional Text. Therefore we can conclude that the Traditional Text was one underlying text for the Latin Vulgate.

Coptic (Egyptian) Christians in their Sahidic translation (predominant in southern Egypt) and their Bohairic translation (predominant in northern Egypt) followed other Greek texts early on; but according to Hills (pg.88), eventually new editions began to move toward support of the Traditional Text.

By the Middle Ages (500-1500 AD) the Traditional Greek Text was the commonly accepted text. **This acceptance of the Traditional Text is why the early English translations noted above were based on it. The reason the Latin Vulgate was consulted was because the Traditional Text was largely employed by Jerome to produce it.** Where Greek manuscripts were missing certain sections of Scripture, the Vulgate could serve as a valuable source of textual readings.

It is significant, then, to recognize and emphasize that the Traditional Greek Text is the text that clearly found acceptance among Christians from the 4th century forward—and all the English translations, up to and including the King James Version, were from that text. It should be noted that the 1611 Edition of the King James Version underwent modifications, yielding new editions over many years, until the work of Benjamin Blayney, published in 1769, produced our present King James Version. However, still underlying the King James Version was the Traditional Text.

Questioning the Origin of the Traditional Text

Today some scholars have little regard for the Traditional Text, though it had been the accepted text for so many years. They teach that although it became the accepted text among Christians, it could not represent the original writings of the New Testament. Many believe (in harmony with a theory proposed by Hort in his *The New Testament in the Original Greek: Introduction,* pg.137) that the Traditional Text originated between 250 and 350 AD. They contend it was created by Christian scholars, who met in a Council in Antioch, Syria, and that Lucian of Antioch (c. 250-312 AD) may have been the original leader of the effort. They believe this created text sometimes matched other texts, sometimes combined two readings from different texts, or took readings and modified them in some way. The supposed goal of the Council was to establish a compromise text, which could gain official status to thence replace all other texts. It has been noted by objective observers however, **that no historical record of such a Council exists.**

In spite of the lack of historical support, these scholars still support the theory that the Traditional Text was a late text, being completed around 350 AD. It supposedly, therefore, never existed until that time. The scholars believe the Council used other Greek Texts that already existed to create the new text. Gathering manuscripts they would take one reading from one manuscript for a particular verse/text, take another reading for another, sometimes combine verses, or sometimes modify a verse/text.

Preliminary Thoughts on the Age of the Traditional Text

As a preliminary response to Hort's theory on the origin of the Traditional Text, it would be helpful if someone could identify distinct Traditional Text readings in manuscripts that existed before the conceived Council at Antioch. If the Traditional Text can be shown to have existed before the middle of the 4th century, the theory of those who reject it is seriously called into question. Can this be done?

Edward Miller took up the task. Miller wrote *A Guide to the Textual Criticism of the New Testament* (1886). John Burgon (1813-1888), an advocate for the Traditional Text, had created a massive index of quotations from the Church Fathers, citing them 86,489 times. In his work, Miller only considered quotations from those Church Fathers who had died before 400 AD. Miller's conclusion was that the quotations of the Church Fathers supported the Traditional Text 2,630 times, compared to support for what has been called the Neologian text 1,753 times. (The Neologian text was the text edited by Westcott and Hort mentioned above.) Even more significant from Miller was the conclusion that if only earlier Church Fathers are considered, from Clement of Rome (2nd half of 1st century) to Irenaeus (2nd half of 2nd century) and Hippolytus (1st half of 3rd century), the comparison of 151 to 84 is even more supportive of the Traditional Text.

While some offer arguments to try to diminish the number of distinct Traditional Text readings from these quotations; what they cannot do, is disprove the existence of the Traditional Text before the 4th century. **In other words, there is no way the Traditional Text was produced later, at some 4th century Council of Christian scholars. It clearly existed very early in Church history. This important information is determinative in the whole manuscript/version issue.**

What motivated Westcott and Hort to reject the Traditional Text?

As noted, the Traditional Text had been the accepted Greek text by Christians for hundreds of years. It is fair to consider what motivated Tischendorf and Tregellus, followed by Westcott and Hort, to reject it.

Westcott and Hort stand at the end of a long list of men who, for a number of reasons, sought to undermine the confidence of God's people in the Traditional Text. Some were no doubt sincere believers, but rejection of the text appears to have been built on the foundations of Rationalism and Naturalism. A representative list of men and their views is given below, which will demonstrate the development of antagonism toward the Traditional Text.

Hugo Grotius (1583-1645)

Grotius was a Rationalist. He took the naturalist approach in criticism, saying basically that all judgment of truth can be made via reason. He made no distinction between the Bible and other works. He made conjectural emendations to the text— restructuring the text to correct what he saw as errors. Grotius' view, that no distinction should be made between the Bible and other works, became foundational to the work of Westcott and Hort.

John Fell (1625–1686)

Fell suggested that variants in manuscripts (deviations/ disagreements) should cause the critic to focus on the scribes who copied the text, rather than focus on the original authors. He espoused the view that comparing various kinds of scribal errors could allow one to detect and eliminate false readings. Fell opened the door to the genealogical approach to textual criticism.

Richard Bentley (1662–1742)

Bentley advocated rejection of the current Greek text and Traditional manuscripts, in favor of constructing a new text based on comparison of the oldest Greek manuscripts and the Latin Vulgate. Some writers say he considered Codex A (Alexandrinus) to be the *oldest and best manuscript in the world*. It is dated 5th century and is Byzantine (Traditional Text) in the Gospels; but follows the Vulgate in some books, and Sinaiticus and Vaticanus elsewhere. Codex Alexandrinus was to be his main source; but he selected 7 other manuscripts also, which were mainly Byzantine.

Bentley advocated conjectural emendation, as did Grotius. In *The Text of the New Testament,* 4th edition, pg.227, Bruce Metzger says that Bentley depended on his *own instinctive feeling as to what an author must have written.* To rewrite portions of the Bible based on instinctive feeling is a scary method of editing. Perhaps we can be glad he never finished his work.

Bentley is called the Founder of Historical Philology. Philology is the study of historical writings to discover their authenticity and original form.

Johann Bengel (1687-1752)

It is believed that Bengel was the first to propose the theory of families of manuscripts. Bengel is also mentioned by some writers as a strong advocate for Codex A.

He established 17 rules for textual criticism. He is especially recognized for the rule which states, *The harder reading is to be preferred to the easier reading.*

Generally his rules also included:

- Preference of the ancient manuscripts to the later

- Low regard for conjectures

- High regard for Church Fathers

- Preference for those readings from various geographical locations

- Rejection of obvious corruption

- Selection of those readings with intrinsic quality

- Usage of Grammatical/Historical rules

A major issue of concern is that his theory of the harder reading being preferred to the easier reading implied that **true** believers intentionally changed their own scriptures.

J.S. Semler (1725-1791)

Semler is viewed as the Father of German Rationalism. He declared, "The whole of Revelation must be brought to the bar of reason." If something is *unreasonable,* it should be rejected.

Semler was the first to reject equal value of the Old Testament and the New Testament. He rejected the uniform authority of all parts of the Bible. He rejected the Divine authority of the traditional canon. He rejected equal inspiration of all Scripture. He rejected identifing Scripture as Revelation. He claimed Scripture *contained* the Word of God rather than *being* the Word of God. He followed Bengel in classifying manuscripts into families.

J.J. Griesbach (1745-1812)

Griesbach was a Rationalist Theologian and pupil of J.S. Semler. He was the first to identify manuscript families by name—The Western Text type, The Alexandrian Text Type, and the Byzantine Text Type. He claimed the Gospel of Mark was an uninspired compilation of Matthew and Luke.

He established 15 rules for textual criticism.

1. The shorter reading is better than the longer.

2. The harder and more obscure is preferred to the plain.

3. The harsh—ungrammatical, non-customary, offensive, and idiomatic—is to be preferred over the pleasant and smooth.

4. Unusual, rare words or rare usages are to be preferred over the common.

5. The less emphatic readings are to be preferred over the one with greater vigor.

6. Those readings less in support of piety are to be preferred over those supportive of piety.

7. Where meaning of a reading appears false, but discovered to be true to be; it should be preferred.

8. A strong orthodox reading is suspect.

9. Preference should go to the middle ground where readings are mixed.

10. Readings where definition or interpretations seem to appear are suspect.

11. Repeated words or sentences are suspect.

12. Readings that may have come from (been inserted by) Church Fathers are suspect.

13. Readings that may have come from Lectionaries are suspect.

14. Readings that may have been brought over from Latin are suspect.

15. Obvious copyist errors are to be rejected.

Karl Lachmann (1793-1851)

Lachmann was the first major editor to break from the Received Text in favor of the Alexandrian Text. He used the genealogical approach of textual criticism to write an edition of Lucretius. He showed how 3 main manuscripts all derived from one arch type. This approach became central in the Westcott and Hort theory of textual criticism.

Samuel Tregelles (1813-1875)

Tregelles is noted as being theologically conservative. He rejected the Received Text as being based on later manuscripts. He published a new version of the Greek text of the New Testament, based on *ancient* manuscripts and the Church Fathers. His work paralleled the work of Karl Lachmann, whom he later met. He worked closely with Tischendorf and visited him to examine Sinaiticus.

He was a member of the committee overseeing the preparation of the English Revised Version. The ERV is often promoted as a work of Westcott and Hort, who are the best known committee members. Tregelles was a major influence on Westcott and Hort.

Constantine Tischendorf (1815–1874)

Tischendorf was influenced by Lachmann to depart from the Received Text. He discovered the Sinaiticus manuscript.

His critical principles included:

- Use of only ancient evidence—Greek manuscripts—Church fathers

- Reject readings from only a single witness

- Reject obvious copyist errors

- Consider parallel passages suspect, especially in the Gospels

- In comparisons of readings, prefer those that seemingly give occasion to other readings

- Consider the context and the style of writers

Brooke Foss Westcott (1825-1901)

He was a teacher of Hort at Cambridge, where they began a lifelong friendship. With Hort, he co-authored *The New Testament in the Original Greek*, also known as the Westcott and Hort Text. The text was based heavily on the critical works of Tischendorf and Tregelles.

Fenton John Anthony Hort (1828–1892)

In 1881, along with Wescott, he published a critical edition of the New Testament entitled *The New Testament in the Original Greek*.

He theorized that Vaticanus, Sinaiticus, and a few other *early* manuscripts, formed what he called the Neutral Text—that is, the text with the least corruption.

Based on their Greek Text, as members of the large committee mentioned earlier, they translated the English Revised Version of the Bible. It was promoted as a revised edition of the King James Version and made over 30,000 changes. What is significant is that those 5,337 changes were made as a direct rejection of the Greek Received Text (TR), in favor of readings from other Greek texts. These changes are monumental since there are only 7,956 verses in the whole New Testament.

The influence of Rationalism and Naturalism took its toll on both Westcott and Hort. Out of these *movements*, arose the view that the Bible should be put on a par with ancient classics. For the purpose of textual criticism or any other reason, to put the Bible on par with any other book for any reason opens the door to confusion and error. These movements also contributed greatly to the development of critical methods to evaluate the biblical text.

What data has been available to New Testament critics?

In the search to identify the original wording of the New Testament, the critics have had a great deal of material to consider.

The earliest New Testament manuscripts are known as the Papyri, because they were written on Papyrus. They are dated as early as c. 200 AD and as late as c. 275 AD. They are very important; but there are very few of them, and none of them are complete New Testaments. The next grouping of New Testament manuscripts were written on Vellum (prepared animal skin—leather). The oldest of these were written in Uncial letters (capital letters). There are over 260 Uncial Manuscripts; they are dated up to around the 10th century. In the 9th century minuscule handwriting came into usage. *Minuscule* means small letters. This style of writing developed into what we call cursive writing. There are over 2750 Minuscule Manuscripts. They are dated from the 9th to the 16th century and make up most of the existing New Testament Manuscripts.

In addition to the actual Greek New Testament Manuscripts, there has been discovery of Lectionaries. Lectionaries are books (lists) having sections of the Greek New Testament divided for the purpose of Scripture readings in early Church services. There are over 2100 Lectionaries. Also scholars have been aided by quotations of early Church Fathers. Finally, there has been examination and evaluation of translations of the Greek text into other languages.

Over 5,000 manuscripts of the Greek New Testament have been recovered. Some of them are complete copies of the New Testament; while some are so small they contain only parts of a couple of verses. They have been found in a variety of locations. As we might expect there are many differences found among the manuscripts. Some of the differences can be definitely ascribed to misspellings and careless work by copyists, but scholars believe that most of the New Testament variations were made deliberately.

Beginning around 1550, Stephanus began to evaluate and catalogue the manuscripts. Since that time, many have taken up the task, including Brian Walton in the 1600s; John Mill in the 1700s; C. Tischendorf, J.J. Wettstein, J.M. Scholz, F.H.A. Scrivener, S.P. Tregelles, and John.W. Burgon in the 1800s. Familiar names from the 1900s include C.R. Gregory, Kirsopp Lake, H. C. Hoskier and Kurt Aland. This list is far from exhaustive. The work of these and others has been the task of evaluating and comparing the manuscripts, ultimately **seeking to identify, as closely as possible, an accurate rendering of the original Greek New Testament writings.**

How did the critics propose to use the available data to make their case for identifying the text of the original New Testament manuscripts?

In the 1700s Johann Bengel (1687–1752) proposed the theory of families of Greek manuscripts. Johann Semler (1725–1791) followed Bengel's theory and suggested that all the Greek manuscripts could be put in one of three families. J.J. Griesbach (1745–1812) refined these ideas and was the first to identify three families by name. The families were described as Text Types and were defined by grouping together those manuscripts with similar characteristics in their readings. Within each family, while there are many differences among the manuscripts, it was believed there was enough commonality to unite them as a *Family* and to distinguish one family from another. The families were designated as the Western Text Type, the Alexandrian Text Type, and the Byzantine Text Type (Traditional Text). Manuscripts representing the Alexandrian Text Type are relatively few. Manuscripts representing the Byzantine Text Type number in the thousands.

The existence of these families of manuscripts became critical to Hort's theory regarding the ability to identify the original text of the New Testament. The theory claimed that the *genealogy of each family* could be ascertained by analyzing and comparing the available manuscripts. Theoretically (and simplistically), the idea was to discover a manuscript of one Text Type—let's say Alexandrian. By comparing it with others, one could find differences and similarities to see if the others were also of the Alexandrian Text Type. For instance, when manuscripts shared variants (deviations/alternate readings) they would be assigned to the same Text Type. When a group of manuscripts were identified as Alexandrian; they would be compared with each other to judge which ones were to be dated earlier and which were later. Using the ancestor (the earlier) as a basis for more comparison and analysis of manuscripts, one could identify an even earlier ancestor. The theory proposed that by continuation of this genealogical process, one could work back through the manuscripts, sift out errors, establish an ancestral line, and eventually identify the original text or that text which was closest to the original.

As we noted above in our list of men, there were whole lists of rules established to guide this work of Textual Criticism. This theory was fully introduced into New Testament Textual Criticism by Hort in the mid 1800s, though it was the position held earlier by Constantine Tischendorf (1815–1874). It had actually been used with other ancient writings, by Karl Lachmann (1793-1851), who applied it to various copies of the ancient classic Lucretius.

The Westcott and Hort Perspective

As we have stated, the Traditional Text had found acceptance with believers for hundreds of years. Then, two Greek manuscripts were discovered that were dramatically different from the Traditional Text. One was Codex Vaticanus. It had actually been known and kept in the Vatican Library since 1481. At some point in the mid 1800s it was fully transcribed, and scholars realized how much it varied from the Traditional Text. The other manuscript was Codex Sinaiticus which was discovered by Tischendorf in 1844, in the Monastery of St. Catherine on Mount Sinai. Both of these manuscripts have been dated to the 4th century and were classified as belonging to the Alexandrian Text Type. Vaticanus is dated as early 4th century and Sinaiticus is dated as mid to late 4th century.

In his book, *The King James Version Defended*, Edward Hills writes on page 65, *In the 1860s **Aleph** (Sinaiticus) and **B** (Vaticanus) were made available to scholars through the labors of Tregelles and Tischendorf, and in 1881 Westcott and Hort published their celebrated Introduction in which they endeavored to settle the New Testament text on the basis of new information. They propounded the theory that the original New Testament text has survived in almost perfect condition in these two manuscripts, especially in **B**(Vaticanus).*

Hort declared in *The New Testament in Original Greek*, pg.225, *It is our belief that the readings of Sinaticus and Vaticanus should be accepted as the true readings until strong internal evidence is found to the contrary and that no readings of Sinaiticus and Vaticanus can safely be rejected.*

These two manuscripts, as noted above, were classified as being of the Alexandrian Text Type, which was Tischendorf's favored. So on the basis of the *new information* ie, their access to Aleph and B, Westcott and Hort claimed that the New Testament text issue was resolved. They proposed that the original New Testament text had survived in almost perfect condition. Their declaration represented a total rejection of the Traditional Text, which meant a rejection of the Byzantine Text type.

Their proposition that in Sinaiticus and Vaticanus and especially in Vaticanus, the New Testament text had survived in almost perfect condition was quite amazing. Herman Hoskier asserts in his work, *Codex B and Its Allies, Volume II*, pg 1, that these two manuscripts disagree with each other over 3,000 times— just in the Gospels. Actually it is 3036 times. That means they average 1 disagreement per verse. How could Hort ignore the significance of these 3036 disagreements, put his stamp of approval on these two manuscripts, and totally reject the text which had been accepted by the church for hundreds of years?

The answer is that he had, under the influence of Tischendorf and Tregelles, developed a bias against the long reverenced majority of manuscripts (The Traditional Text) which served to underwrite the Textus Receptus. Remember, the Textus Receptus was based on the labors of Erasmus, Stephanus, Beza, and the Elzevirs; it was foundational for the translation of the King James Version.

Westcott and Hort's 1881 declaration shook the world of Textual Criticism, but did it have validity and arise out of objectivity?

In Volume I, pg. 211 of Hort's *Life and Letters*, we find a letter from Hort to Rev. John Ellerton, dated December 29-30, 1851. Hort says, *I had no idea till the last few weeks of the importance of texts, having read so little Greek Testament, and dragged on with this villainous Textus Receptus...Think of that vile Textus Receptus leaning entirely on late MSS.; it is a blessing there are such early ones...*

The significance of Hort's letter is paramount in evaluating his work. His rejection of the Received Text was established. Could he proceed with any objectivity? Earlier in the same letter to Ellerton, Hort referenced the work of Bagster, Scholz, and Tischendorf, and no doubt had their work in mind when referring to the blessing of early manuscripts. Their work promoted the *early* manuscripts, namely Sinaiticus and Vaticanus, which would eventually become available to Hort.

Constantine Tischendorf was a Naturalist who had previously concluded that the perceived Alexandrian Text Type was the best, while the Textus Receptus was from late and inferior manuscripts. Hills (pgs. 225-226) writes that by the middle of the 19th century, Tischendorf and Tragelles had convinced many British scholars that the lateness and inferiority of the

TR, demanded a revision of the King James Version. As noted earlier, a committee was appointed by the Church of England, with **one of the most influential members of the New Testament group being Fenton A. J. Hort.**

The first key point in understanding the efforts of Westcott and Hort was their belief that, since the manuscripts used in editing the TR only went back to the 12th century (possibly the 8th), the Text Type itself must have been of later origin and therefore inferior. Their conclusion that Vaticanus and Sinaiticus best represented the original text of the New Testament, meant there was not much need for their genealogical method to be applied to the Byzantine (Traditional) Text, or for that matter, to any other text.

Hort's Theory Regarding the Transmission of the Text

Hort not only followed the thinking of Tischendorf regarding favorability toward Vaticanus and Sinaiticus, he also followed him when it came to his view of the Bible and Textual Criticism. Tischendorf, as a Naturalist, held a secularist view of the Bible, especially when it came to Textual Criticism. He believed the Bible should be treated as any other ancient book. We noted this view as going all the way back to the Rationalist, Hugo Grotius. All three of these men (Grotius, Tischendorf, and Hort) ignored the spiritual nature of the Bible, and evidently ignored the conflict that had raged over the Word of God, going all the way back to the beginning of human history in Genesis. Other ancient books are not the object of spiritual attack. These men ignored devilish attempts to corrupt the text of the Bible on the one hand, and ignored any providential work of the Lord in preserving the text on the other. They denied the uniqueness of the Bible and the unique demands placed on the work of handling the sacred text.

Hort advocated the position that the New Testament was to be treated like any other book, and then further declared that he believed there were no signs of **deliberate falsification** of the biblical text **for dogmatic purposes**. Think about that! Was he not aware of the significance of John's message in the book of Revelation when he wrote, *For I testify unto every man that heareth the words of the prophecy of this book, If any man shall add unto these things, God shall add unto him the plagues that are written in this book: And if any man shall take away from the words of the book of this prophecy, God shall take away his part out of the book of life, and out of the holy city and from the things which are written in this book.* (Revelation 22:18-19) Who would dare to think that no one ever intentionally endeavored to change the scriptures for **dogmatic** purposes?

Whether Hort actually believed his own declarations is unknown, but his naturalistic view of the Bible opened the door for him to advance the theory of a genealogical approach to text evaluation. This naturalistic approach might work well with ancient classic texts, as used by Lachmann to edit Lucretius—but, who would try to twist and change Lucretius? A huge majority of errors in copies of an ancient classic would immediately be assumed to be mistakes. Finding an error in one copy and then finding the same error in another copy would make it easy to relate the copies to each other. The error made in one might easily have been continued in the next. One could conceivably sift through such errors and find his way back to the original.

So, Hort promoted the idea that there was a *normal transmission* of the biblical text through the years that it had been passed from one copy to the next. Variants (deviations) were simply mistakes made by copyists. How important was the belief in normal transmission of the text? **The genealogical approach to textual criticism was totally dependent on normal transmission of the text.**

However, when one faces the assertion of Ernest Colwell in *What is the Best New Testament?* pg.53, that **the majority of variant readings in the New Testament *were* created for theological or dogmatic reasons**, everything changes. Hort's whole approach to Textual Criticism was based on his assertion that Scripture enjoyed normal transmission from copy to copy without any *deliberate falsifications.*

H. H. Oliver addressed Hort's theory in his article, *Present Trends in the Textual Criticism of the New Testament*, published in *The Journal of Bible and Religion, XXX* (1962). He said, *The W-H theory is much like a multistoried building—each level depends on the one below it. Thus Hort's simplistic notion of 'genealogy' absolutely depends upon the allegation that there was no deliberate alteration of the text, and his notion of 'text types' absolutely depends upon 'genealogy' and his arguments concerning... readings... depend upon those 'text types'. The foundation for the whole edifice is Hort's position that the New Testament was an ordinary book that enjoyed an ordinary transmission. With its foundation removed, the edifice collapses.*

Oliver's point was clear. If there was ever deliberate alteration of the biblical text, one could not simply use the genealogical approach and sift his way back to the original New Testament writings. Deliberate insertions and changes along the way would totally distort the concept of an ancestral line leading back to the wording of the original text. The theorized Text Types were established by a supposed ancestral line. It was the common variants (deviations) that put manuscripts into the same Text Type. Without an ancestral line, each manuscript must stand alone and be individually analyzed and evaluated. There would be no basis for establishing a *family* relationship.

A second key point in understanding Westcott and Hort's efforts is to realize they believed there was a normal

transmission of the Greek text from copy to copy. In other words, while they acknowledged the presence of inadvertent errors, they denied there was ever any intentional effort to change the text for dogmatic or doctrinal purposes. Therefore they thought they could legitimize the family tree (genealogical) approach in Textual Criticism.

It was in the proposition of the genealogical approach to the Scriptures, ignoring the spiritual nature of the Bible, denying intentional efforts to corrupt it, and therefore espousing normal transmission of the text, which paved the way for Hort's use of Text Types to undermine respect for the Received Text (TR).

Hort's Handling of Text Types

At this point, Hort's view of Text Types (Families), which had originated with Griesbach, becomes very significant and worthy of consideration. Imagine the task of taking over 5,000 individual manuscripts and beginning to evaluate, analyze, and classify them. It would first of all require that manuscripts be catalogued. This would include documenting the writing material (Papayri, Vellum, etc.), the style (Uncial, Minuscule, etc.), the date, and also establishing a system for identification (P75, Codex D, etc.). On page 117 Hills reports that this work was actually started in the 1550s by Stephanus; who, using the Traditional Text as his primary source, printed his 3rd edition of the T.R. and placed in its margin variant readings from 15 manuscripts. In our day, thousands of manuscripts have now been included in a basic system of cataloguing. That however only begins the work. Once a manuscript has been catalogued, it must be studied to understand what it says. Then it must be compared with other manuscripts to identify the variant readings. If you have an accepted text, such as was used by Stephanus, all variants would be compared to the primary text.

While Hort accepted Griesbach's identification of 3 ancient Text Types (the Alexandrian, the Western and the Byzantine [Syrian]), his prior position on the Alexandrian Type totally affected his actual work of textual evaluation. Remember, he had already concluded that the Alexandrian Text Type was best, and that Vaticanus and Sinaiticus represented the original New Testament text in near perfect condition. Therefore he apparently ignored any need for the long, agonizing work, which would be required to consider and analyze all existing manuscripts. In fact, there is no record to show that Hort's method of genealogical textual evaluation was ever applied in practice. There seems to be no notes from such a work and no charts to reveal the results of him tracing the family tree of any manuscripts. He basically declared the existence of the proposed Text Types, as if they were identified through the genealogical process.

A major problem for Hort was the huge majority of Byzantine (Traditional Text) manuscripts. He had to account for them and diminish their significance. After all, there were thousands of them. They had been accepted as best representing the original. The work of Erasmus, Stephanus, Beza, and the Elzevirs was respected and English versions of the Bible had come from them.

With the genealogical theory available, though never apparently used to any degree, Hort was able to justify accepting the concept of Text Types. He initially named 4. In taking the thousands of manuscripts and placing them under 4 different headings (now identified as 3: the Alexandrian, Byzantine, and Western), he could diminish the significance of any single manuscript. Suppose there were 20 manuscripts—15 might be considered Byzantine, 3 as Alexandrian, and 2 as Western. Rather than evaluate all 20, he could simply reduce them to 3 *witnesses*. The 15 Byzantine became one witness to that proposed type. The 3 Alexandrian became one witness to that proposed type, and the 2 Western became one witness to that proposed type. Whatever work of comparison and evaluation he did would simply pit the Types against each other, not manuscripts against each other.

Having already concluded that the so called Alexandrian Text Type was the best and that Vaticanus and Sinaiticus represented an "almost perfect" original New Testament text; he simply had to find a way to destroy people's confidence in the Byzantine (Syrian) Text Type in general, and the Textus Receptus in particular. Through the use of Text Types, he eliminated the impact of thousands of Byzantine (Traditional Text) manuscripts—many of which, have apparently never yet received full analysis. Though they stood as a huge majority of witnesses to the history of the text, he grouped them, and only counted them as one corporate witness.

Ernest Colwell writes on page 158 of his *Hort Redivivus,* that *Hort organized his whole argument to depose the Textus Receptus.* That seems to tell the story.

A third key point in understanding Westcott and Hort's efforts is to realize that while they sought to legitimize the genealogical approach to Textual Criticism, they apparently never actually applied it in practice. The work that was intended to establish and identify Text Types was by-passed, but the concept of Text Types became a tool to undermine the Traditional Text.

What about Text Types?

Here is a question. Do text types, as Hort espoused them, actually exist? Kurt Aland, in *The Significance of the Papyri,* pgs. 334–337 in discussing the discovery of the Papyri writes, *The simple fact that all these papyri, with their various distinctive characteristics, did exist side by side, in the same ecclesiastical province, that is, Egypt, where they were found,* **is the best argument against the existence of any text types**... *the increase of the documentary evidence and the entirely new areas of research which were opened to us on* **the discovery of the papyri, mean the end of Westcott and Hort's conception.**

Frederick Kenyon in his *Handbook to the Textual Criticism of the New Testament* says the so called Western text type is *not so much a text as a congeries (collection) of various readings.* His point (also held by others) is that there never was a single manuscript of that *type* that could have been designated as an original. In other words, it would be impossible to trace the manuscripts back to any starting point.

Hills quotes M.M. Parvis, from his article, "The Nature and Task of New Testament Textual Criticism," printed in *The Journal of Religion, XXXII* (1952), pg. 173. *We have reconstructed text-types and families and sub-families, and in so doing, have created things that never before existed on earth or in heaven...when we have found that a particular manuscript would not fit into any of our nicely constructed schemes, we have thrown up our hands and said that it contained a mixed text.*

Aland, Kenyon, Parvis, and others raise doubts about the existence of Text Types. What is the significance of those doubts? As we have noted, the reality of Text Types is dependent on the genealogical method of text evaluation. That is how Text Types would be identified. The genealogical method of text evaluation is validated only if there was normal transmission of the text. In other words, the whole theory presented by Hort rises or falls on whether there were ever attempts to intentionally corrupt the text of the Bible. Beyond theory, however, is the very likely scenario that Westcott and Hort never did the work that would have supposedly vindicated their views.

There are over 5,000 Greek manuscripts to be considered in the search for the original wording of the New Testament. Though some have not been completely evaluated, it appears that no two manuscripts match with perfect exactness. If narrowly defined text types do not exist to aid in the process of manuscript evaluation, how are answers derived in search of the original?

Beginning at the beginning

Let the reader be reminded at this point that our intent is not to enter into details of textual criticism. Many experts have taken up the task and have written volumes upon volumes to present and defend their views. Their writings are extensive and detailed, often representing a lifetime of effort. The challenge for us on a *pastoral* level is to guide our people in making decisions about the use of Bible versions—availing ourselves of the views of the experts, while facing the reality that in textual criticism (as in every other area of life and ministry) the experts disagree. They all have the same facts; but, for a variety of reasons, they arrive at different conclusions in interpreting the facts. As noted at the outset of this brief study, our purpose is to introduce the issues of the debate and to demonstrate why a strong minority of Bible believers are not willing to accept the newer Bible versions.

So, rather than plunge any deeper into the battle of the experts, let's consider a possible scenario which would have produced the manuscripts which we have available.

The New Testament was originally written in the Greek language. We call those original writings the Autographs. The books of the New Testament were written over a period of about 50 years. Most believe James was the first of the New Testament writings and is generally dated around 45 AD. The last book of the New Testament to be written was Revelation, dated generally around 95 AD. None of the Autographs (the actual writings of the New Testament writers) have ever been found. They no doubt got worn out through usage.

However, in Eusebias' *Church History*, the record of Gaius, a Roman churchman from late in the second century (writing about 175-200 AD), reveals his challenge to four heretics (Theodotus, Asclepiades, Hermophilus, and Apollonides) who corrupted the biblical text. Each did his own work, so their corruptions differed from the true text and from each other. The challenge from Gaius was for them to *produce the originals from which they made their transcripts*. The question has been posed. Could Gaius have so challenged them, if he could not produce originals to prove them wrong? **It is fair to conclude that at least some of the Autographs were still existing and in the hands of the faithful until near the end of the 2nd century A.D.**

From the Autographs, Christians made handwritten copies of the biblical text for continual usage for the local believers and for distribution to others. Paul made it clear in Colossians 4:16, that he expected that letter to be made available to others. He writes, *And when this epistle is read among you, cause that it be read also in the church of the Laodiceans; and that ye likewise read the epistle from Laodicea.* Whether this encouragement was related to the actual original writing or to copies being made and forwarded is not certain, but all agree the copying work started early.

At some point in history there were efforts to alter the biblical text. While there surely were some errors in the work of copying the text, scholars agree that most variants found in Bible manuscripts were intentionally created. It is believed the departures from the true text began during the 2nd century A.D. and probably ended before the beginning of the 3rd century A.D. The corruptions exposed and challenged by Gaius are perfect examples.

Note the commentary of some of our experts:

Colwell writes in *The Origin of Text Types*, pg. 138—*The overwhelming majority of readings were created before the year 200.*

Scrivener writes in *A Plain Introduction to the Criticism of the New Testament,* 4th edition, Vol.2, pg. 264—*It is no less true to fact than paradoxical in sound that the worst corruptions to which the New Testament has ever been subjected, originated within a hundred years after it was composed.*

Zuntz writes in *The Text*, pg.11—*Modern criticism stops before the barrier of the second century; the age, so it seems, of unbounded liberties with the text.*

G. D. Kilpatrick writes in "The Transmission of the New Testament and its Reliability, " printed in *The Bible Translator, IX* (July 1958), pgs. 128-9, that the creation of new variants ceased by about 200 AD.

Kilpatrick writes in *Atticism and the Text of the Greek New Testament,* pgs.129-30—*From the early third century onward the freedom to alter the text which had obtained earlier can no longer be practiced. Tatian is the last author to make deliberate changes in the text of whom we have explicit information. Between Tatian and Origen Christian opinion had so changed that it was no longer possible to make changes in the text whether they were harmless or not.* (Tatian, 120-180 AD / Origen, 184–253 AD)

To this point in our discussion, let us agree that at least some, and maybe all, of the Autographs were in the hands of the faithful near the end of the 2nd century AD and that attempts to corrupt the text had begun and ended by that same time. In other words, corruptions of the true text could be identified and exposed up to 200 AD.

A Proposed History of the New Testament Text

Wilbur Pickering, in his book, *The Identity of the New Testament Text,* laid out his view of the history of the New Testament text. Without reproducing it word for word, but endeavoring to represent his presentation and credit him with the work, we will follow his theory. It is based on much clear history, coupled with logic and sound argument.

How were the New Testament writings viewed in Apostolic times? This is important in our study, because Hort claimed that textual purity attracted hardly any interest. He claimed there was no evidence that care was taken to choose out for transcription the exemplars having highest claims to be regarded as authentic. His claim would be significant, if true; but was it true?

Consider the writers themselves.

Paul wrote in I Corinthians 14:37, *If any man think himself to be a prophet, or spiritual, let him acknowledge that the things that I write unto you are the commandments of the Lord.* That is a strong statement. Consider his bold assertion in I Corinthians 2:7-13, that God had revealed truth to him and that the Holy Spirit had guided him in teaching it. Read also II Corinthians 10:7-8, Galatians 1:6-12, and II Thessalonians 3:12-14. In admonishing Timothy in I Timothy 5:18, he combines Luke 10:7 with Deuteronomy 25:4, calling both Scripture.

Peter clearly equated his own writings with the prophets in II Peter 3:2. Then in II Peter 3:15-16, he equates Paul's epistles with the *other* Scriptures.

Consider the view of others in Apostolic times.

Clement of Rome used the Scriptures in his letter to the Corinthian church. He referred to Hebrews 12:6 as *the holy word*, along with reference to Psalm 118:18. He ascribes the biblical book of I Corinthians to Paul, saying it was written *with true inspiration*. This bishop of the church at Rome, writing about 96 AD, seemingly quoted from Matthew, Acts, Titus, James, and I Peter and definitely quoted from I Corinthians, Romans, and Hebrews.

The Epistle of Barnabus uses the familiar reference to the Scriptures of our Lord Jesus, *as it is written*, when quoting Matthew 20:16 and/or Matthew 22:14.

Let it be recognized that New Testament writers viewed their own work as Scripture and their contemporaries viewed the New Testament writings as Scripture. Would these early believers who had held the Old Testament in such high regard, not honor these new revelations of God's truth with the same reverence?

How did the faithful of the 2nd century view the New Testament writings?

As the second century unfolded in church history, the view of New Testament writings was meaningful. Were the writings viewed as authoritative? Indeed, were they viewed as Scripture?

Polycarp wrote to the church at Philippi (c. 115 AD). It is noted that he quoted or clearly alluded to the New Testament writings at least 50 times. Pickering references a translation of "The Fathers of the Church" by Francis Glimm (found in Glimm's work, *The Apostolic Father*) where Polycarp says, *I am sure you are well trained in the sacred Scriptures...Now it is well said in these scriptures, 'Be angry and sin not, and let not the sun go down upon your wrath.'* Here Ephesians 4:26 is quoted.

The 2nd letter of Clement of Rome (c. 150 AD), after quoting from the Old Testament, says, *Another Scripture says, 'I came not to call the just, but sinners.'* This statement of the Lord Jesus is found in Matthew 9:13, Mark 2:17, and Luke 5:32.

Justin Martyr in his dialogue with Trypho, says in Trypho119, that just as Abraham believed the voice of God, *in like manner, we having believed God's voice spoken by the apostles of Christ.* In Trypho 81 he writes, *And further, there was a certain man with us, whose name was John, one of the apostles of Christ, who prophesied, by a revelation that was made by him, that those who believe in our Christ would dwell a thousand years in Jerusalem.*

Athenagorus in his *Plea* written in 177 AD quotes Matthew 5:28 as Scripture when he says, *We are not even allowed to indulge in a lustful glance. For, says the Scripture, 'he who looks at a woman lustfully, has already committed adultery in his heart.'*

Pickering lists the comments of others including the Shepherd of Hermes, Melito, Bishop of Sardis, Theophilus, Bishop of Antioch and more. Finally is the commentary regarding Irenaeus and his work, *Against Heretics* (c. 185 AD). The commentary says, *Irenaeus stated that the apostles taught that God is the Author of both Testaments. (IV, 32.2) and evidently considered the New Testament writings to form a second canon...From the time of Irenaeus on there can be no doubt concerning the attitude of the Church toward the New Testament writing—they are Scripture.*

Let it be noted, that not only did the apostles and their contemporaries view the New Testament writings as Scripture, but the Church Fathers of the 2nd century AD also reverenced these writings as the Word of God.

Did the early church care about the text?

Hort argued there was little concern for textual purity in the early church. Is that view supported by the evidence? Pickering makes an important opening statement on the matter (pg.100) when he says, *Starting out with what they knew to be the pure text, the earliest Fathers did not need to be textual critics. They had only to be reasonably honest and careful.*

We know the apostles were very concerned about the text. They warned of false teachers as seen in many New Testament references. Peter explicitly warned of those who would wrest (twist) the Scriptures to their own destruction (II Peter 3:16). And we have already quoted the solemn warning of Revelation 22:18-19, which concluded the book and concluded the entire New Testament writings. Let us quote it here again to demonstrate that neither the Lord nor His servants of the early church would tolerate any tampering with the very Word of God.

> *For I testify unto every man that heareth the words of the prophecy of this book. If any man shall add unto these things, God shall add unto him the plagues that are written in this book: And if any man shall take away from the words of the book of this prophecy, god shall take away his part out of the book of life, and out of the holy city, and from the things which are written in this book.*

Pickering adds another statement (pg.101) which has bearing on the matter. Basing his view on the letters of Ignatius and the conclusion from those letters that there was a great deal of communication between the churches of Asia Minor, Greece, and Rome, Pickering proposes *that a problem with a heretic in one place would soon be known all over.*

But, did anybody care? Listen to Polycarp (7:1), *Whoever perverts the sayings of the Lord...that one is the firstborn of Satan.* I think he took it seriously. In Trypho xxxv Justin Martyr said that the fact that heretics were teaching doctrines of the spirits of error, *causes us who are disciples of the true and pure doctrine of Jesus Christ to be more faithful and stedfast in the hope announced by Him.* Pickering also tells of Dionysius, bishop of Corinth (168-176), who complained that his own letters had been tampered with—and worse yet, the Holy Scriptures also.

Against Heretics was a work of Irenaeus written about 180 AD. Irenaeus was a disciple of Polycarp, who was a disciple of the Apostle John. *Against Heretics* was written in opposition to Gnosticism. Notice Irenaeus' reverence for and confidence in the Scriptures. He said that the doctrine of the apostles had been *handed down by the succession of bishops, being guarded and preserved, without any forging of the Scriptures, allowing neither addition nor curtailment, involving public reading without falsification.* (*Against Heretics* IV. 32:8)

Irenaeus further showed his regard for the accuracy of the text in defense of a single letter from Revelation 13:18. The debate was whether the text should read 666 or 616. He defended the 666 rendering saying that it was found *in all the most approved and ancient copies* and that *those men who saw John face to face* bear witness to it. He went on to warn that *there shall be no light punishment upon him who either adds or subtracts anything from the Scripture* (XXXI). I think Irenaeus took the matter just as seriously as Polycarp. At this point in time, Irenaeus was Bishop of Lyons in southern France. It seems he did not have the Autographs, but did have absolute confidence in the ancient copies available to him and had no time for anyone who would make the slightest change in the text.

On the other hand, we wonder if the Autographs were still being read in the early third century in the churches to which they were sent. Tertullian had warned of the danger of spiritual curiosity, which would take one outside the Scriptures. In his *Prescription Against Heretics* XXXVI, he writes, *Come now, you who would indulge a better curiosity, if you would apply it to the business of your salvation, run over the apostolic churches, in which the very thrones of the apostles are still pre-eminent in their places, in which their own authentic writings are read, uttering the voice and representing the face of each of them severally. Achaia is very near you (in which) you find Corinth. Since you are not far from Macedonia, you have Philippi; (and there too) you have the Thessalonians. Since you are able to cross Asia, you get Ephesus. Since, moreover, you are close to Italy, you have Rome, from which there comes even into our own hands the very authority (of apostles themselves).* He challenged heretics to measure their beliefs by the Word of God. He obviously cared about the purity of the Scriptures.

Contrary to Hort's view, it is clear that early Church Fathers had a high view of the Scriptures and a commitment toward maintaining the integrity of the text.

What about the Transmission of the Text?

It is clear that the New Testament writings were immediately regarded by believers as the written Word of God. Reverence for those writings continued as the church grew in number, and as it spread through the preaching of the gospel and missionary church planting efforts. It is apparent that copies of the text were made, so churches could have their own copy of the New Testament for their ministry. Justin had written that the memoirs of the apostles were read each Sunday in the assemblies. That could only happen if they had the Scriptures. As copies were made there was great concern for their purity, and repugnancy toward any effort to modify or corrupt the text. All these things are clear from the evidence we have reviewed.

Pickering asks (pg.104), *But were all the faithful equally situated for transmitting the true text?* He answers his own question. *Evidently not.* Then he makes a statement that is marked by simplicity, but profound in importance. He said, *The possessors of the Autographs would obviously be in the best position.*

Who possessed the Autographs?

Pickering argues: *Speaking in terms of regions, Asia Minor may be safely said to have had twelve (John, Galatians, Ephesians, Colossians, I and 2 Timothy, Philemon, I Peter, 1 and 2 and 3 John, and Revelation; Greece may safely said to have had six (1 and 2 Corinthians, Philippians, 1 and 2 Thessalonians, and Titus in Crete); Rome may safely said to have had two (Mark and Romans)—as to the rest, Luke, Acts, and 2 Peter were probably held either by Asia Minor or Rome; Matthew and James by either Asia Minor or Palestine; Hebrews by Rome or Palestine; while it is hard to state even a probability for Jude, it was quite possibly held by Asia Minor. Taking Asia Minor and Greece together, the Aegean area held the Autographs of at least eighteen (two thirds total) and possibly as many as twenty four of the twenty seven New Testament books; Rome held at least two and possibly up to seven; Palestine may have held up to three...*

Pickering finishes the sentence with these words, ***Alexandria (Egypt) held none.*** *The Aegean region clearly had the best start and Alexandria the worst.*

Let us pause in our discussion of transmission to note that the typical Textual Critic claims that the earliest extant manuscripts are the best, which leads to the acceptance of Hort's position on Vaticanus and Sinaiticus. But let us further note the following from Pickering pgs.116 -117 where he states, *It is common knowledge that all the earliest MSS, the ones upon which our critical texts are based, **come from Egypt**. When the textual critic looks more closely at his oldest manuscript materials, the paucity (small quantity) of his resources is more fully realized. All the earliest witnesses, papyrus or parchment, come from **Egypt** alone. Manuscripts produced in **Egypt** ranging between the third and fifth centuries, provide only a half-dozen extensive witnesses (the Beatty Papyri, and the well known uncials, Vaticanus, Sinaiticus, Alexandrinus, Ephraem Syrus, and Freer Washington.)* Pickering takes this information from Kenneth W. Clark's, *The Manuscripts of the Greek New Testament*, pg.3. Pickering adds that the Bodmer Papyri must now be included and goes on to say, *But what are Egypt's claims upon our confidence? And how wise is it to follow the witness of only one locale? Anyone who finds the history of the text presented herein to be convincing will place little confidence in the earliest MSS.*

Returning to the discussion of transmission, Pickering argues, *On the face of it, we may reasonably assume that in the earliest period of transmission of the N.T. text the most reliable copies would be circulating in the region that held the Autographs.*

Pickering goes on to present his case that the most dependable copies of the text would originate in the places that held the Autographs, because accuracy could be easily assured. False wording would be immediately exposed, while true wording could be verified. Producing these validated copies would be done to meet the needs of the growing body of believers and the growing number of localities being reached with the gospel. Pickering writes (pg.106), *By the early years of the second century the dissemination of such copies can reasonably be expected to have been very wide-spread, with logical consequence that the form of text they embodied would early become entrenched throughout the area of their influence.*

He goes on to declare that the process just described would establish a trend that would continue *inexorably*—that it would be prohibitive for a text form so entrenched to ever be dislodged from its dominant position by a competing text form, no matter how many generations of manuscripts there might be. He claims it would take an extraordinary upheaval in transmissional history to ever open the door to an aberrant text form, and that no such upheaval is ever recorded in history.

Claiming the copying process of validated texts had gotten underway quite early, Pickering writes (pg.107), *It follows that within a relatively few years after the writing of the N.T. books there came rapidly into existence a 'majority' text whose form was essentially that of the Autographs themselves. This text form would, in the natural course of things, continue to multiply itself and in each succeeding generation of copying would continue to be exhibited in the mass of extant manuscripts.* He finalizes his thoughts on this point by averring, *So then, I claim that the N.T. text had a normal transmission, namely the fully predictable spread and reproduction of reliable copies of the Autographs from the earliest period down through history of the transmission until the availability of printed texts brought copying by hand to an end.*

So it is, we have today a Majority Text, which while rejected by the critics, stands as a testimony to its own validity. It is the result of the normal and expected transmission of faithful copies of the original New Testament writings from the Apostolic times until the arrival of the printing press. It stood up to the challenges of aberrant text forms from the 2nd century and continued to expand in number and influence.

How do we explain the existence of Vaticanus, Sinaiticus, etc.?

We have already demonstrated the concern of early believers regarding corruption of the text. We have also noted that it is believed that major efforts to change the text began during the 2nd century A.D. and ended before the beginning of the 3rd century A.D. These efforts apparently were accepted in local areas for a time; but they could not find permanent or widespread acceptance, because the Autographs or virtually exact copies of the Autographs were available for comparison. Pickering states (pg.110), *Although a bewildering array of variants came into existence, judging from extant witnesses, and they were indeed a perturbing influence in the stream of transmission, they would not succeed in thwarting the progress of normal transmission* (of the majority text form).

Pickering goes on to make the case, that as challenged earlier, there were no competing text types in the earliest years of the church and no major recensions. He says (pg.110), *We may expect a broad spectrum of copies, showing minor differences due to copying mistakes, but all reflecting one common tradition. The simultaneous existence of abnormal transmission in the earliest centuries would result in a sprinkling of copies, helter-skelter, outside of that main stream...We have the Majority Text...Traditional Text, dominating the stream of transmission with a few individual witnesses going their idiosyncratic ways...There is just one stream, with a number of small eddies along the edges.*

To help us understand his point, he reminds us that there is no competing text type with the majority, because in fact, (pg.112), *The minority MSS disagree as much (or more) among themselves as they do with the majority.*

On page113 Pickering tells us, *The inconsistent minority of MSS...are remnants of abnormal transmission of the text, reflecting ancient aberrant forms.*

Hence the popular and oft referenced Vaticanus and Sinaiticus, which as noted earlier disagree with each other over 3,000 times in the Gospels, should not be thought of as the *most ancient and best*. Nor should they be thought to follow a common text type. Nor should they be thought to represent the original New Testament text in near perfect condition. Rather it seems they each represent individual efforts to revise the New Testament text, but failed to ever displace the majority of manuscripts which were descendants of the Autographs. They are deemed to be of the **Alexandrian Text Type**, because **Egypt** is where manuscripts of similar character can be traced.

Of course there is great disagreement with the conclusions drawn regarding the Majority Text. We will make a few more comments on surrounding issues, but the Traditional Text stands up well to the tests of its character and historicity. No one will go wrong in following it and in continuing to use the King James Version.

Some added thoughts and clarifications.

1. The argument in favor of Vaticanus and Sinaiticus was that they were the oldest and best manuscripts that existed. However, the fact that a particular manuscript is oldest does not mean that the text recorded in it is necessarily the oldest or the best. Having survived for hundreds of years may likely suggest a manuscript was not used and, in fact, unworthy of use. For instance, Papyrus 66, one of what is called the Bodmer Papyri, was found in 1952 and dated c. 200 AD, making it one of the oldest New Testament manuscripts ever to be found. It contains almost all of the Gospel of John.

After studying P66, Colwell observed (*Scribal Habits*, pgs.378-9) that it had what he called 200 nonsense readings, 400 itacistic readings (inconsistent spellings), and 482 readings found in no other manuscript. And that was just in the Gospel of John. It was old, but very bad work. Should it be accepted based on its age?

2. In harmony with our previous statement, the reason older manuscripts of the Traditional Text have not been found, may be because they were used and thereby became worn out. Once copies were made to replace the worn out copies, there was no need to save the worn ones.

3. We also need to briefly revisit the challenge offered by Pickering, where he said (pg.117), *But what are Egypt's claims upon our confidence?* We have yet to find rationale for believing that Alexandria somehow became the center for *guarding* the biblical text. **Egypt** certainly had no claim to any of the Autographs. Yet, all of the earliest manuscripts, including Vaticanus, Sinaiticus, and the Papyri, come from **Egypt** and nowhere else.

4. The actual existence of the Alexandrian family of texts (text type) has been questioned, with the suggestion that all of the manuscripts found in **Egypt** are so different from each other that they should be viewed as individuals. Now I know that we need to be careful to not necessarily condemn someone's work on a given topic, just because he does not believe exactly what we believe. With that said, however, it is often pointed out that the first New Testament critic to classify manuscripts into families by name, was a 19th century German Rationalist named Johann Griesbach. Griesbach was a faithful student of Johann Semler,

who is considered the Father of German Rationalism. My reading tells me that Griesbach was an enemy of Orthodox Christianity, who denied the Deity of Christ, denied the infallibility of Scripture, and denied the inspiration of the Gospel of Mark, claiming it was a compilation of Matthew and Luke. With his text type theory at the very heart of New Testament textual criticism, should we really put any stock in his views?

5. One more issue needs emphasis. Hort adopted the idea that the Bible should be viewed as any other ancient book. This approach to the Bible denies the uniqueness of the Bible as the Word of God and ignores obvious intent to corrupt the Book by the enemies of the faith. However, to view the Bible as any other ancient book is foundational to Hort's genealogical approach to text evaluation. Recognition of the uniqueness of the Bible calls Hort's entire theory into question.

What has modern textual criticism produced?

At the very beginning of this study, we noted that in recent years there has been the publication of an avalanche of English versions. They have come from a minority of Greek manuscripts and often have been translated using an eclectic method of text/reading selection. For a while one version would be popular, then another would take its place, soon to be followed by another. Today, the version of choice by more and more churches and schools is the English Standard Version or as it is usually called—the ESV.

This is not an exhaustive evaluation of the ESV, but it will reveal why there is so much concern about it (and other versions) among Bible believing Christians. It has eliminated some precious readings that we find in the King James Version, which is based on the Traditional text. At first, the significance of these changes is written off as *not being found in the 'oldest and best' Greek manuscripts.* But what does that mean? If these many readings found in the King James Version, which was based on the Traditional Text, were not found in what is now claimed to be the best manuscripts, where did they originate? Since most of these readings are stronger and more honoring to the Lord than those found in the ESV and the minority Greek texts, the implication must be that it was orthodox scribes, who at some point decided to intentionally and arbitrarily add readings to the Greek text of the New Testament. In other words, the corruption of Greek manuscripts is to be blamed on the true believers. I would think intentional corruption of the text would be the work of unbelievers—wouldn't you?

Let's illustrate some differences of the ESV from the KJV.

Verse Elimination:

In Mark 15:28 the King James Version says, *And the scripture was fulfilled, which saith, And he was numbered with the transgressors.* **The ESV eliminates the verse.**

In John 5:4 the King James Version says, *For an angel went down at a certain season into the pool, and troubled the water: whosoever then first after the troubling of the water stepped in was made whole of whatever disease he had.* **The ESV eliminates the verse.**

In Acts 8:37 the King James Version says, *And Philip said, If thou believest with all thine heart, thou mayest. And he answered and said, I believe that Jesus Christ is the Son of God.* **The ESV eliminates the verse.**

The ESV completely eliminates 17 verses from the New Testament.

Verse Portions Deleted:

In Luke 9:55-56 the King James Version says, "But he turned and rebuked them, *and said, Ye know not what manner of spirit ye are of. For the Son of Man is not come to destroy men's lives, but to save them.* And they went to another village." **The ESV deleted what we have put in italics.**

In John 8:59 the King James Version says, "Then took they up stones to cast at him: but Jesus hid himself, and went out of the temple, *going through the midst of them, and so passed by."* **The ESV changed some words and deleted what we have put in italics.**

In Hebrews 2:7 the King James Version says, "Thou madest him a little lower than the angels: thou crownest him with glory and honor, *and didst set him over the work of thy hands."* **The ESV deleted what we have put in italics.**

In Matthew 9:9 the King James Version says, "And I say unto you, Whosoever shall put away his wife, except it be for fornication, and shall marry another, committeth adultery: *and whoso marrieth her which is put away doth commit adultery."* **The ESV deleted what we have put in italics.**

The ESV deleted portions of many Bible verses.

Verse Portions Changed:

In I Timothy 3:16 the King James Version says, *And without controversy great is the mystery of godliness:* **God was manifest in the flesh,** *justified in the Spirit, seen of angels, preached unto the Gentiles, believed on in the world, taken up to glory.*

The ESV changed the verse to read, "Great indeed, we confess, is the mystery of godliness: **He was manifested in the flesh**, vindicated by the Spirit, seen of angels, proclaimed among the nations, believed on in the world, taken up to glory."

In Luke 2:33 the King James Version says, *And **Joseph** and his mother marveled at those things which were spoken of him.*

The ESV changed the verse to read, "And **his father** and his mother marveled at what was said about him."

In Hebrews 2:16 the King James Version says, *For verily he took not on him the nature of angels; but **he took on him the seed of Abraham.***

The EVS changed the verse to read, "For surely it is not angels that he helps, but **he helps the offspring of Abraham.**"

Salvation Confusion in the ESV

The ESV brings unnecessary confusion to the salvation message by its rendering of the present articular participles found in a number of verses.

In Acts 2:47 the King James version says, *Praising God, and having favor with all the people. And the Lord added to the church daily **such as should be saved.***

The ESV renders it, "**those who were being saved.**"

In I Corinthians 1:18 the King James version says, *For the preaching of the cross is to them that perish foolishness; but **unto us which are saved it is the power of God.***

The ESV renders it, "**to us who are being saved** it is the power of God"

In I Corinthians 15:2 the King James Version says, *By which also **ye are saved**...*

The ESV renders it, "by which **you are being saved...**"

In II Corinthians 2:15 the King James Version says, *For we are a sweet savour of Christ, in **them that are saved**...*

The ESV renders it, "For we are the aroma of Christ to God among **those who are being saved**..."

The present articular participle is found in many places in the New Testament. A simple illustration of how translating it with continual action brings confusion can be seen in John 11:26. Our Lord Jesus said, *And whosoever liveth and believeth in me shall never die. Believest thou this?* To take the same translating approach as the ESV uses in the verses above would require this rendering of John 11:26. "Whosoever keeps on living and keeps on believing in me shall never die."

In fact, the present articular participle is not determinative of whether an action described is continuous or not. The rendering of *being saved* in the verses noted above is not necessary and only brings confusion. It is worth noting that the ESV does not use a continuous action translation in John 11:26. It says, "And everyone who lives and believes in me shall never die. Do you believe this?" Shame on the ESV editors!

Precious Names and Titles Removed by the ESV

In a cursory review of the ESV, it was discovered that numerous verses were missing the term *Lord, Jesus, Christ, Jesus Christ,* or *Lord Jesus Christ*. To be fair it should be acknowledged that in some verses the term *Jesus* or *Christ* was found in the ESV while not in the KJV. An exhaustive review reported by Dr. Terry Watkins from Dial-the-Truth-Ministries, claims that the ESV removes *Jesus* 18 times, *Jesus Christ* 51 times, *Christ* 39 times, *Lord* 66 time, and *God* 38 times. The New Testament message is surely undermined by this weakening of testimony to our Savior.

What Conclusions Can We Draw from this Study?

We begin by stating that we can find no justifiable reason for the critics to have ever called into question the validity of the Traditional Text—other than the assumption, that since the extant Byzantine manuscripts could be dated no earlier than the 8th century A.D., the text of those manuscripts must be late and inferior. The assumption, however, had no basis in fact. We have demonstrated that the age of a particular manuscript may have little bearing on its quality.

Second, a foundational weakness in the approach of Westcott and Hort to Textual Criticism is the assertion that the Bible should be treated as any other ancient book. As a Christian, who sees clearly in Scripture the ongoing attack against the Word of God, we cannot accept Hort's position that there were *no signs of deliberate falsification of the biblical text for dogmatic purposes.* With our rejection of that concept, comes a rejection of the entire Westcott and Hort theory; because their theory ultimately depends on a normal transmission of the text and that did not happen.

Third, we find ourselves wholeheartedly agreeing with the reasonableness of Pickering in advancing the concept that those regions (Asia Minor, Greece, Palestine) which received the Autographs of the New Testament letters were in the best position to guard the accuracy of copies; whereas, **Egypt** (where the minority texts originated) was in the worst position to guard the accuracy of copies.

Fourth, the clear implication of the critic's view of variant readings lays the blame for corruption of the text on the true believers. Since the Majority Text has stronger readings in support of biblical truth than the minority, the believers are held to be guilty of defying Scripture by adding to the Word of

God. We realize than an overzealous scribe might be foolish in a particular instance, but we reject the supposition that the practice became common and produced thousands of variant readings.

Fifth, we accept the reasonable explanation for the development and expansion of the Majority Text, to the point that it established and maintained dominance over all aberrant manuscripts that were written and offered to the early believers.

Sixth, we have deep appreciation for the Textus Receptus and the King James Version of the Bible, though we attribute no measure of inspiration to either of them.

Seventh, because all modern versions are based on minority manuscripts, we reject them. Excellent translation of the wrong text or easy reading of a tainted version does not well serve the church or the individual Christian.

Eighth, the King James Version does have some archaic words, but rather than trade it in for the confusion and error of an ESV or some other modern version, the serious student of the Word can easily learn the meaning of a difficult term. Besides, sometimes the ESV uses terms that are more difficult to grasp than those in the KJV. For instance in Matthew 1:11 the KJV uses *carried away*, the ESV uses *deportation*. Which is easier? In Matthew 8:11 the KJV uses *sat,* the ESV uses *recline at table*. Which is easier? In Mark 2:21 the KJV uses *new,* the ESV uses *unshrunk*. Which is easier?

Finally, we believe the Majority Text is superior to the minority texts and we believe the King James Version still stands as the best representative of the original New Testament Text, but—

Does it matter?

There is a cavalier attitude toward the Word of God today, as never before. One pastor in addressing the issue of a modern version said, "It is still the Word of God, isn't it?" A leader in the Conservative Evangelical movement of today said it did not matter, because he was sure that if someone read, believed, and obeyed any of the modern versions they could get saved and know how to live. We think it does matter when a text is selected that diminishes the truth.

When in Luke 2:43, the ESV changes *Joseph and his mother* to read *parents*, does it matter? The ESV rendering undermines the virgin birth and Christ's deity. Some will excuse this disgraceful way of handling God's Word, by saying these truths are taught elsewhere; but the writers of God's Word had purpose in their choice of words, which must not be dismissed or ignored. When the ESV takes the warning of II Timothy 3:3, that in the last days, men shall be *without natural affection* and waters it down to read *heartless*, does it matter? The ESV rendering destroys one of the most serious warnings of God to His people as we face the last times.

We need an awakening to the sanctity of God's Word. God has exalted His Word above His name. Our Lord Jesus made it clear that every jot and tittle will be fulfilled. Today we walk on dangerous ground. Undermining what God said, marked the beginning of Satan's spiritual war on earth. We find no reason to think that war has stopped.

Reference Materials

Aland, Kurt. "The Significance of the Papyri for Progress in New Testament Research."

The Bible in Modern Scholarship. ed. J.P. Hyatt. New York: Abingdon Press, 1965.

Analytical Greek Lexicon. London: Samuel Bagster and Sons Ltd., 1967.

Burgon, John William. *The Revision Revised.* 1883. Reprint from The Bible For Today, Collingswood, NJ, 1984.

Cloud, David. *Is the Received Text Based on a Few Late Manuscripts?* Port Huron, MI, Fundamental Baptist Information Service, 2000.

Colwell, Ernest Cadman. *Hort Redivivus: a Plea and A Program*, Leiden: E. J. Brill, 1969.

"Scribal Habits in Early Papyri." *The Bible in Modern Scholarship.* ed. J.P. Hyatt. New York: Abingdon Press, 1965.

What is the Best NewTestament? Chicago: The University of Chicago Press, 1952.

"The Origin of Text types of New Testament Manuscripts." *Early Christian Origins,* ed. Allen Wikgren. Chicago: Quadrangle books, 1961.

Dana, H.E. and Mantey, Julius R. *A Manual Grammar of the Greek New Testament.* Toronto: The Macmillan Co., 1957.

Hills, Edward F. *The King James Version Defended.* Des Moines, Iowa: The Christian Research Press, 1956; Reprint 1988.

Hort, Arthur Fenton. *Life and Letters of Fenton John Anthony Hort*. 2 vols. London: Macmillan and Co., Ltd., 1896.

The New Testament in the Original Greek: Introduction. London Macmillan, 1896.

The New Testament in the Original Greek. New York: Harper Brothers, 1882.

Hoskier, Herman C. *Codex B and its Allies.* 2 vols. London: Bernard Quartich., 1914.

Kenyon, F. G. *Handbook to the Textual Criticism of the New Testament.* London: Macmillan, 1912.

Kilpatrick, G.D. "Atticism and the Text of the Greek New Testament." *Neutestamentliche Aufsatze.* Regensburg: Verlag Friedrich pustet, 1963.

"The Transmission of the New Testament and its Reliability." *The Bible Translator, IX.* (1958).

Lovegrove, Bill. *The Bible Text and Translation Debate.* PilgrimWorks.com, 1999.

Metzger, Bruce M. *The Text of the New Testament.* London: Oxford University Press, 1964.

Miller, Edward. *A Guide to the Textual Criticism of the New Testament.* London: George Bell and Sons, 1886.

Oliver, H.H. "Present Trends in the Textual Criticism of the New Testament." *The Journal of Bible and Religion.* XXX (1962).

Parvis, Merrill M. "The Nature and Task of New Testament Textual Criticism." *The Journal of Religion.* XXXII (1952).

Pickering, Wilbur N. *The Identity of the New Testament Text.* Nashville: Thomas Nelson Inc., Publishers, 1977.

Robertson, A. T. "The Epistles of Paul." *Word Pictures of the New Testament.* Nashville: Broadman Press, 1931.

Scrivener, F. H. A. *A Plain Introduction to the Criticism of the New Testament.* 4th ed. Edited by E. Miller. 2 vols. London: George Bell and Sons, 1894.

Stauffer, Douglas D. *One Book, One Authority.* Millbrook, AL: McCowen Mills Publishers, 2012.

Stitterly, Charles Fremont. *Text and Manuscripts of the New Testament.* Bible researcher.com, Reprint from ISBE, 1929.

Tertullian. *The Prescription Against Heretics.* Translated by Rev. Peter Holmes, reprint from Early Christian Writings.

Tobin, Paul. "New Testament Manuscripts and Text Types." *The Rejection of Pascal's Wager.* 2000.

Watkins, Terry. *The Truth About the English Standard Version.* Dial The Truth Ministries.

Wilken, Bob. "The One Who Believes…" *Faith Alone* (mag). 2006.

Williams, J. B (Editor). *From the Mind of God to the Mind of Man.* Greenville: Ambassador-Emerald International, 1999.

Wuest, Kenneth. *Word Studies in the Greek New Testament.* Grand Rapids: Wm. B. Eerdmans Publishing Co., 1953.

Zuntz, G. *The Text of the Epistles.* London, Oxford University Press, 1953.

*other data gathered from Wikipedia articles on text types, miniscules, uncials, lectionaries, and papyri.

PARENTING
ONE CHANCE
TO DO IT
RIGHT!

E. ALLEN GRIFFITH

Allen Griffith has written a book for parents that offers hope! Based on Biblical principles his guidance and encouragement, along with *practical helps*, will lead parents toward a Christ honoring approach in training their children.

$12.95, paperback, 156 pages.
Available in Christian bookstores or contact info@FLPublishers.com
ISBN: 978-0-9749836-3-9 (Spring Arbor)

Biblical Family Ministries
www.biblicalfamilyministries.org

Faithful Life Publishers
www.FLPublishers.com

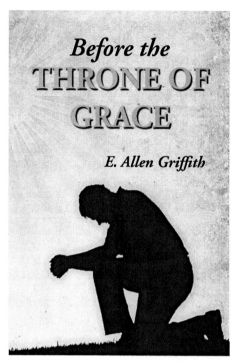

Before the
THRONE OF
GRACE

E. Allen Griffith

No greater privilege has been proffered mankind than the solemn opportunity to step personally into the Throne Room of Heaven to address the God of the universe in personal conversation. It is utterly amazing that such a privilege has been ignored, abused, misused, and misunderstood by so many.

Don't miss the intended blessings that await the humble saint who comes Before the *THRONE OF GRACE.*

No one is exempt from trouble and heartache.
Trials are common to everyone.

During troubling times, many yield to bitterness and sorrow.
Others find spiritual and emotional victory.

What makes the difference?
Escape from defeat and self pity comes
through knowing and doing what the Bible says.

Those who really want victory can have victory.

PAPERBACK EDITION:	HARDCOVER EDITION:
Available at Christian book stores around the country.	Available through Biblical Family Ministries
ISBN: 978-0-9749836-9-1 (Spring Arbor distributors)	ISBN: 978-0-9749836-0-8 122 pages • $13.95
128 pages • $11.99 FaithfulLifePublishers.com	BiblicalFamilyMinistries.org

CPSIA information can be obtained at www.ICGtesting.com
Printed in the USA
BVOW03s1413270813

329569BV00006B/18/P